Published by
Carpe Diem Publishers

P.O. Box 2146
San Benito, TX 78586
806-433-6321

www.carpediempublishers.com

Printed in the United States of America

ISBN: 975-1-949215-22-9

Preface

Telling this story was enjoyable because it is a true story with a cheerful ending. Rubi is a chihuahua and terrier mix that survived ten sweltering days and nights in the wooded countryside of east Texas near the city of Crockett.

After being launched from our vehicle due to a severe car crash, Rubi darted out into the woods to hide because she was frightened and confused. While I was airlifted to the hospital, Rubi made her way to a nearby barn at the home of Dan Craven DMV and his wife Michelle. Over the next few days, they occasionally spotted Rubi running here and there on their property but could not catch her. Michelle left food and water for her and responded to a lost dog post I had on Facebook, letting me know that they had seen her.

Over the next 9 days, many friends helped search for Rubi by foot, car and four-wheeler, and putting up flyers. On the tenth day, the Cravens texted that they had seen her again. A close friend raced me out to the Craven home and there I spotted her walking out of the hot pasture.

I'm not sure what she endured those 10 days alone, but with so many predators, I had almost given up hope. This story is about what I imagine happened while she was out there. Surprisingly, she was uninjured, only having bug bites, scratches and being thin and dirty.

Amber Larke Stone

Special thanks
to Moms' sister
Robin Collins
for graphic layout
and editing.

This book is
dedicated to
Dan and Michelle Craven.

Rubi
A True Story

Written and Illustrated
By Amber Larke Stone

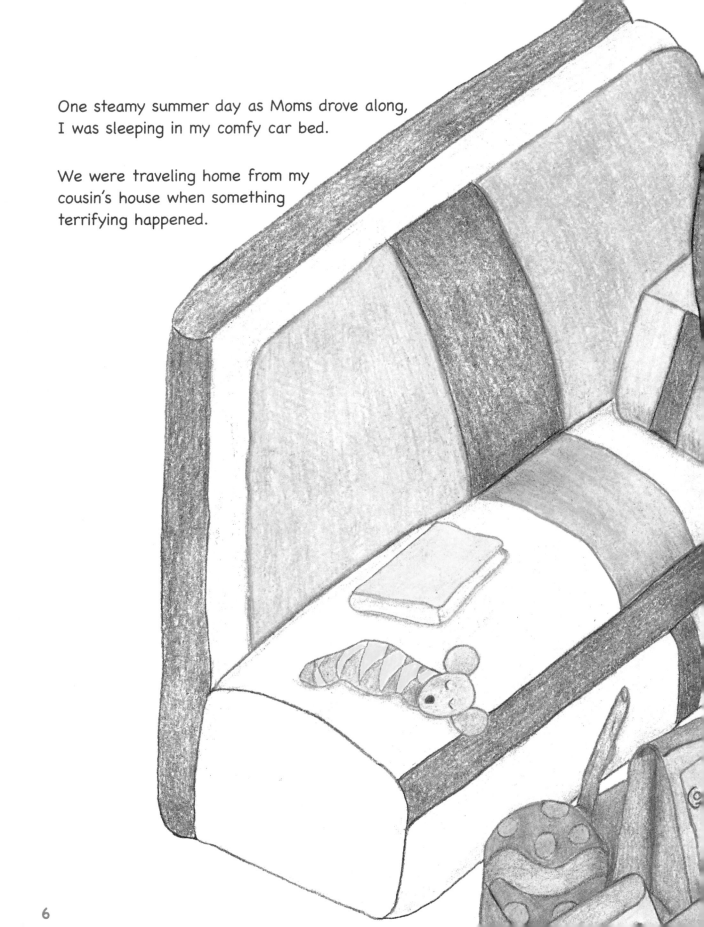

One steamy summer day as Moms drove along,
I was sleeping in my comfy car bed.

We were traveling home from my
cousin's house when something
terrifying happened.

Bam! Boom! Crash!

Suddenly I was tumbling and spinning through the hot, steamy air like a rag doll. With a big smack, I landed on top of a heap of dirt and leaves. Ugh!

When I sat up and looked all around, I realized that I was totally clueless about what had happened or where I was. Worst of all, I could not find my Moms anywhere.

I decided that the logical thing to do was to hightail it away from the chaos around me. So, under a nearby bridge I ran lickety-split. This seemed like the perfect place to rest and wait for Moms to come and find me.

11

After about an hour of waiting, I gathered enough courage to search for Moms. When I came out from under my hideaway, she was gone. No cars, no people, and no Moms. Nothing. Only me and the wilderness.

It was getting dark out here and it was almost bedtime. A safe place to sleep was what I needed to find, so I started walking. Across a creek, up a hill, down a hill and through the tall, scratchy grass I traveled.

I roamed for the longest time. My poor paws were achy and grubby when I eventually found a big, green building that appeared safe and quiet, so I crept in. Not one thing looked or smelled familiar, but it would be good enough for the night. I found a good sleeping spot under a table and curled up.

I was used to snuggling in Mom's cozy bed with my favorite cow toy and blanket. Dog-tired, I finally dozed off. It was a long and restless night.

Meds

CRAVEN DVM

C

FEED

Clackity-clank and bam! I was startled awake by a gigantic door opening loudly. I spotted a strange man coming through the door, so away I scurried. Out the door, under a water trough, past a cow pen, through the itchy grass and into the eerie woods I raced.

The trees seemed similar to the woods at my house, yet everything appeared strange. Being extra cautious, I decided to creep farther into the wooded area to find a secret hiding place where the stranger couldn't find me.

After I rested for a while, I realized that I was super thirsty and getting hungry. Remembering the water trough, I made a trail to it. Fortunately, the trough was low enough for me to gulp down a big, long drink of water.

Food was more difficult to find. I noticed the cows in the pen were gathered in a circle eating, so I decided to join them.
They were not as friendly as I expected.
They quickly chased me away.

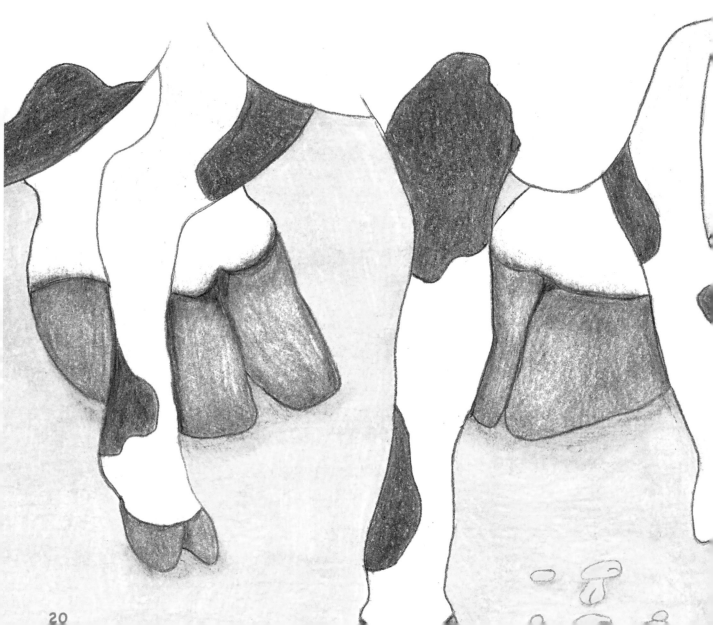

I went back to the big green building and what luck! I found animals that were my size and friendly. They also had food and did not mind sharing it.

Each day I followed my trail to the water trough, into the big green building for food and then back to the woods to wait for Moms.

Nighttime in the woods was spooky and terrifying. It was extremely dark, and I heard many unusual noises. Oodles of bugs were everywhere, and I couldn't get away from them. Some of them were most peculiar and they crawled on me all night while I tried to sleep.

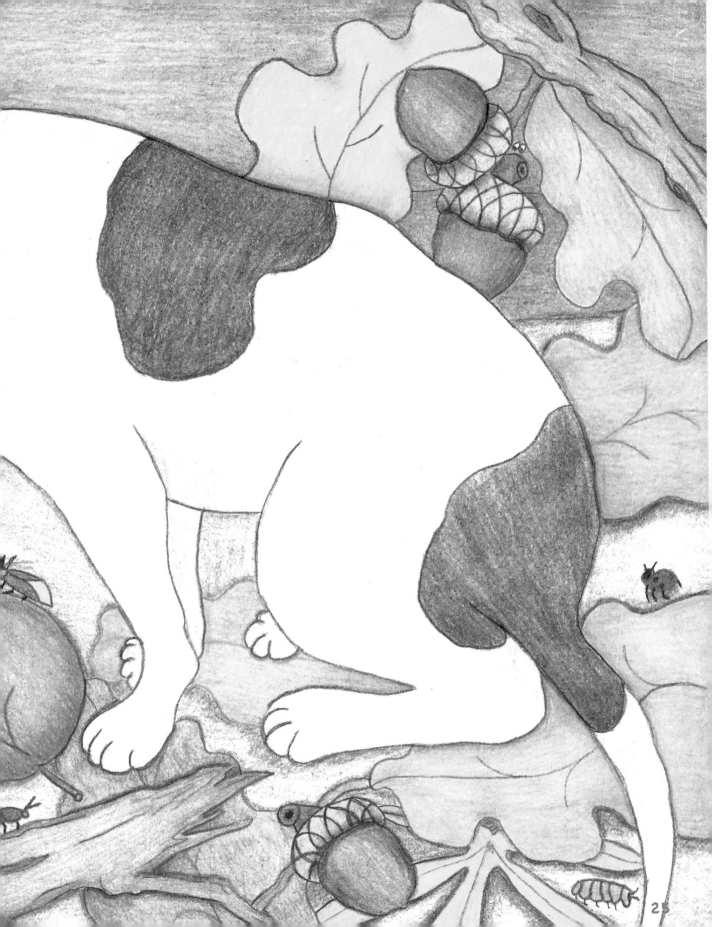

One night, I spotted a very long creature that didn't have any teeth and was scary. It wiggled and slithered through the leaves and stuck its tongue out at me as it slid past.

The next night, I spied a spiky varmint that waddled through the woods near my secret spot. We looked at each other for a minute and it seemed peaceful enough, but wow, that fur looked creepy.

Sniff. Sniff. A night or two after that, I got a whiff of an odor that I had never smelled before. What was this horrid stink and where was it coming from? That is a scent I'll never forget.

Each night the visitors in the woods seemed larger and scarier than the night before. I decided to stay well hidden and out of sight at night. I sure wish Moms was here.

At nighttime, there were all types of buzzing, chirping, chittering and rustling noises surrounding me which made it difficult to sleep peacefully. Most nights I heard the scariest yowling sounds. It sounded like these yappers were very close to me and it was frightening.

Some of the woodsy critters didn't live on the ground.
Looking up in the trees was scary as well.

One day when I was on the grassy trail to the big green building,
I noticed the stranger again. Away I scurried to the safety of the
woods. I waited and watched until the stranger left. When he was
gone, I headed towards the green building for food when I heard
something familiar. Rubi! Rubi! I knew that voice.
It was Moms!

When I glanced around, I couldn't believe my eyes. Moms!
She found me. I scrambled to her as fast as my little sore paws
could run. She grabbed me up and cuddled me closely.
That hug felt so incredibly safe and secure, and I was overjoyed.
Moms clung to me the entire way home. I felt so relieved and happy.

Back at home I got a warm bubbly
bath, a tasty chicken dinner,
and plenty of cool refreshing
water to drink.

I slept for an extra long time. It was such a restful sleep laying in Mom's cozy bed with my toys and blankie. Fortunately, there were no scary critters or pesky, biting bugs. Well, maybe a couple of friendly bugs, but I'm not afraid of them after 10 scary nights in the woods.

Me holding Rubi when we found her.

Dr. Craven.

Rubi, 2 days before she was lost.